Have An Amish Christmas

Dennis Regling

www.visittheamish.com

www.visittheamish.com

The Author
"Mr. Dennis"
Dennis Regling

Amish Christmas

Christmas is the biggest holiday on the Amish calendar, but there's definitely no Santa Claus.

You won't hear the voice of Bing Crosby singing "White Christmas" coming from an Amish kitchen as cookies are being baked for the holidays. Nor will you find the Amish home adorned with the most elaborate display of Christmas lights complete with a decorated tree beaming from the living room window.

All these customs that the English aka "non-Amish," get excited for during the holiday season are considered too extravagant and unnecessary when celebrating Christmas in an Amish household.

Amish Christmas Decorating

That's not to say the Amish do not decorate their homes for the holidays. There is no lavishly decorated Christmas tree in the home. And strings of colorful electric lights do not grace the front of the Amish house.

Greens and candles may decorate some home interiors. Candles are lit and placed in the windows of Amish homes to represent the birth of Christ.

While some Amish families may decorate their homes with Christmas cards from friends and family. Some of the more liberal Amish communities may even decorate with wreaths, stars, angels and garland, but you are not likely to find a Christmas tree or strands of lights in an Amish home.

"The more decorations involved, the less Christ is involved," said Lester Beachy, a new order Amish man and author of *"Our Amish Values."*

Christmas is a very special time in the Amish community. A time to reflect on the true reason for the season.

As might be expected, Amish Christmas customs are simple, oriented to the family and the religious meaning of the holiday. So, Amish children don't visit Santa Claus in the store.

But the making of special cookies and candies is certainly a part of the holiday activities. School children often pick names and exchange small gifts, such as writing paper or a needlepoint kit. Families usually exchange some small gifts as well. Some

Amish also send Christmas cards, often to their "English" friends.

Amish Christmas Service

The Christmas church service may or may not be held on December 25th, but both Christmas and the following day, sometimes called "second Christmas," are holidays for the Amish.

This second day is usually one of relaxation or visiting others. Christmas dinners are a special part of the celebration, These are usually large meals, not unlike those served at weddings, and various groups beside the family will hold get togethers, such as single women, teachers, and others of like interest. These gatherings may continue into January and February of the New Year.

Christmas Morning In The Amish Household

On Christmas morning the family gathers around the head of the household to listen as he reads the story of the first Christmas from the family Bible.

"Our way of celebrating Christmas is to sit and read with the children and tell them the story of how Jesus came to Earth through the Virgin Mary and how he shed

his blood for us on the cross, as a family talk about what Christmas means," said Simon Miller of Clare.

"It has become a tradition in our home, since the Bible has been translated into Pennsylvania-Dutch instead of just German (or English), that we like to read the Christmas story in our Pennsylvania-Dutch dialect," said Beachy.

Just like any other day, the cows must get milked and the horses must be fed. The family heads out to take care of the chores and then they reconvene for breakfast.

Amish Christmas Gifts

Finally, the children are free to open presents as they are presented to them from their parents.

There are no Amish communities that practice the tradition of Santa Claus.

Amish boys and girls will not find the latest gaming devices or other top electronic devices that many non-Amish children will receive this Christmas. Instead, younger children will receive wooden toys, model toy tractors or books and handmade dolls.

Contrary to popular belief, a large majority of Amish children play with dolls with faces. This tradition of faceless dolls may still be prominent in more conservative, old order Amish communities.

Boys and girls may also receive sporting equipment such as softball gloves and bats, and croquet and volleyball sets. Family oriented games like board and card games are highly encouraged in Amish families and make great gifts. Beachy and his family enjoy engaging games of Dutch Blitz and Uno; two popular card games among the Amish community.

"In our community, we object to gaming devices. We want families to be together more," said Beachy. *"We Discourage gaming devices as it disrupts family time."*

This can vary from church district to church district. It would not be uncommon to see an Amish child playing with a battery operated gaming device, it would simply depend on the church they are a part of.

Older Amish men and women would most likely receive gifts that are practical in nature and can be used in their homes or on the farm. Women may receive household items such as quilts and china while the men may receive tools for their farm or shop.

"One year I got a stepladder," Simon Miller said. *"The children get clothes or something they need."* Younger children may also receive a second gift, perhaps a toy or storybook,"* he added.

Christmas Dinner In The Amish Home

The traditional Christmas dinner is usually the highlight of the Christmas celebration.

The Christmas meal is usually quite elaborate including roasted chicken, mashed potatoes and gravy, stuffing, salads, fruits, breads, cakes, cookies, pies and candies.

Each family tends to have their own Christmas meal and gathering and with Amish families being so large, these gatherings can last well into February.

"It's not easy to get the entire family home for the holidays. Especially with many living in other states," said Beachy.

Other Christmas Traditions:

Amish communities may have many different customs and traditions depending on the community they live in. Each community is different, but their message is always the same. Christmas is a time for Christ.

A Christmas program is usually planned at the schoolhouse each year. Amish children will put up decorations, sing songs, tell stories, read poems and put on plays in order to celebrate the meaning of Christmas.

Homemade treats and gifts such as quilts, toys or other small wooden crafts may be exchanged between the teacher and children. Amish children will continue to go to school throughout the Christmas season without the winter break that many non-Amish children enjoy because their school year is over earlier in preparation for the spring harvest.

The Amish have many non-Amish friends and even family members. Non-Amish visitors may be invited to share in Amish Christmas celebrations which may mean being invited to the school play or attending the family meal. Many Amish and non-Amish people work together and may exchange Christmas cards amongst each other.

Caroling is not just a tradition for the young people in Amish communities. Amish carolers travel to local nursing homes and shut-ins and bring with them gift baskets of homemade goodies like bread and candies to hand out. They visit both Amish and non-Amish care centers.

In Beachy's community, each Christmas the community prepares a list of names of the elderly people in the community and each family is assigned a name. The family prepares something special for that person by making them Christmas cards, gift baskets or other homemade goodies.

Some of the young people in Beachy's community have even created prison ministries. Amish youth travel to different prisons throughout Ohio bringing cards and cookies. They may also share stories and some of their Christmas programs with the inmates.

Overall, the main focus of the Christmas season in the Amish home is to honor and celebrate Christ. While much time is devoted to prayer and scripture, spending time with the family in relaxation and laughter is just as important to the Amish community.

Amish Christmas Songs

The Amish sing traditional Christmas hymns, but special songs are also part of the school programs.

The Amish School Christmas Program

The Christmas programs usually begin with a welcome, sometimes by one of the younger "scholars."

I'm glad it isn't size and weight

And age that counts today,

'Cause then I might not have the chance

To stand up here and say

"MERRY CHRISTMAS!"

While stories are often about their non-Amish neighbors, and may even mention Santa Claus and Christmas trees, clearly this is not what the season represents.

Some of the dialog from the plays suggests the morals behind the stories:

- *"Sometimes the gifts you make bring more happiness than anything you can buy."*

- *"Giving and making others happy is the best part of Christmas."*

- *"The best gift you can give is simply called love."*

Here is a Christmas poem:

This Christmas season let us try

To do some golden deeds,

To carry someone's burden,

To help someone in need.

There are always those who need us

As we journey on life's way,

And the friends we win by helping

Make us richer every day.

So when you see a saddened face

As Christmas time draws near,

Do your best to lift the load

And spread a word of cheer.

In this selection, "Christmas Bees," imagine the seven children walking to the front of the class-room, each holding a bee-shaped "shield" with a word on it. They begin by reciting in unison:

Bees can sting, oh, this is true,

But bees can make good honey, too,

And that's the kind we have for you.

Now each child holds up a word and recites a verse about his or her "bee..."

Be REVERENT in spirit low, at the manger lowly;

And catch anew the vision fair of the Christ Child holy.

Be GENEROUS, give all you can, then give a little more;

Be sure to give more largely now than you ever gave before.

Be THOUGHTFUL of the people who are lonely, old, or sad;

Be thoughtful of the children, too, and help to make them glad.

Be READY quickly to respond to Christmastime appeals;

Be quick to give to friends afar or for the needy's meals.

Be UNSELFISH --- all self-seeking with abandon
cast aside;

Be unselfish --- that's the keynote of the
happy Christmastide.

Be HOPEFUL for the best in life, for hope
has wondrous worth;

It was to bring hope unto men that
Christ came down to earth.

Be APPRECIATIVE for great riches of Christ
and of His love,

And of all the blessings from our Father up above.

Oh, may these "bees" with you abide,

All sweeten well your Christmastide.

The poem, "Ten Little Candles," is to be presented by ten children, each with a lighted candle. Each recites a verse, blowing out his or her candle at the appropriate time.

Ten little candles, Jesus bade them shine,

*But selfishness just snuffed one out,
and there were nine.*

Nine little candles, one without a mate,

*Bad companions came along,
and then there were eight.*

Eight little candles, doing work for heaven,

*"I forgot" sat down on one,
and then there were seven.*

Seven little candles, all with blazing wicks,

*Someone cried out, "Goody Boy,"
and there were six.*

Six little candles, all of them alive,

*But one was tired of playing,
and then there were five.*

Five little candles, once there were more,

Sunday baseball fanned one out,
and then there were four.

Four little candles, bright as bright could be,

But one of them just didn't have time,
so then there were three.

Three little candles, could one of them be you?

That one gave up going to church,
and then there were two.

Two little candles, our story's almost done;

"I'm too small, no use," one cried,
and then there was one.

One little candle, left all alone,

It kept on burning by itself,
and oh how bright it shown.

Brave and steady burned the flame,
until the other nine,

Fired by its example, once again began to shine.

(Now the child with the remaining candle lights the other nine, and the children exit singing, "This Little Light of Mine.")

Christmas Recipe

Take a bit of cheerfulness,

A pinch of laughter, too.

Next take a cup of thoughtfulness,

And stir them through and through.

Now to this add tranquility,

A verse of "Silent Night,"

That ever quiet we may be

When God sends his holy light.

Set aside a moment while you go

For spices, herbs, and pine,

For music, fun, and candle glow,

A star that was the sign.

Then mix and stir and fold again,

And add some mistletoe,

A bit of faith and love and then

Into an oven your cake must go,

Where warmth and affection will combine

To make this cake come true.

Garnish with happiness so fine

Enough for me and you.

Cut a piece, but save some, too,

For each day of the year.

Serve with a prayer of peace on earth,

A heavenly Kingdom near.

In keeping with the focus of the holiday, some Christmas songs and carols are sung. Sometimes new words with a religious meaning are given to secular songs(such as *"Jingle Bells"* or *"Up on the Housetop."*

Even traditional carols may be given new verses, especially for the children.

Here is a re-working of *"O Little Town of Bethlehem."*

O little Inn of Bethlehem

How like we are to you;

Out lives are crowded to the brim

With this and that to do.

We're not unfriendly to the King,

We mean well without doubt;

We have no hostile feelings,

We merely crowd Him out.

The parents, of course, respond enthusiastically to the children. Finally, after all the songs and short skits, the program concludes.

Now that our program's over,

I came to say good-bye,

and what I feel like doing,

Is heave a great big sigh.

Take our mistakes as kisses;

No harm was meant by them.

I hope you did enjoy the day

So you will come again.

"Old" Christmas

Christmas is a time of celebration, feasting and gift-giving throughout the world. And while most people celebrate it on December 25, some Amish communities also celebrate on January 6, or Old Christmas. It's always exactly twelve days after Christmas was the traditional date of the Three Wise Men coming to Bethlehem to find the baby Jesus.

In the Middle Ages, "Old" Christmas the culmination of twelve days of feasting. This is where we get the carol "The Twelve Days of Christmas." December 25 began the feast, which also coincided with the pagan celebration of the winter solstice.

But in 1582, the Julian calendar (based on the phases of the moon) was discarded in favor of the Gregorian calendar by Pope Gregory XIII. After that, throughout Catholic Europe Christmas Day was to be celebrated on December 25.
But the Anabaptist ancestors of the Amish, dissented from these calendar modifications and kept to the Julian calendar, having their celebrations on January 6.

Many Amish have kept this tradition of Old Christmas, even while later adopting the celebration on December 25.

Overall, the main focus of the Christmas season in the Amish home is to honor and celebrate Christ. While much time is devoted to prayer and scripture, spending time with the family in relaxation and laughter is just as important to the Amish community.

Amish ChristmasRecipes

The Christmas season is one of the busiest times in the Pennsylvania Dutch kitchen, where the cookbooks are thrown open and Amish recipes start flying.

For weeks before Christmas the house is filled with the smell of almond cookies, anise cookies, sandtarts, Belsnickle Christmas cookies, walnut kisses, pfeffernusse, and other traditional cookies. Not just a few of one kind but dozens and dozens of many kinds of cookies must be made. There must be plenty for the enjoyment of the family and many holiday visitors.

Amish recipes are all about classic, comforting, and old-fashioned tastes, so it's no surprise that an Amish Christmas dinner menu would feature favorites like meatloaf, potatoes, and fried chicken. If you've got a lot of folks coming over for the holidays, you might want to make a few of these delicious main dishes!

Country Meat Loaf & Potato Casserole

This cozy all-in-one-pan Amish Country Meat Loaf & Potato Casserole is so simple to make, and such a satisfying main dish meal. It fits a busy weeknight or a leisurely familySunday dinner perfectly.

What You'll Need:

- 1 1/2 pounds ground beef
- 1/2 cup chopped onion
- 2 slices white bread, torn into small pieces
- 1 egg
- 1/3 cup ketchup
- 1 teaspoon Worcestershire sauce
- 1/2 teaspoon salt
- 1/2 teaspoon black pepper
- 3 cups seasoned mashed potatoes

What To Do:

Preheat oven to 350 degrees F. Coat an 8-inch square baking dish with cooking spray.

In a large bowl, combine all ingredients except mashed potatoes. Place mixture in prepared baking dish and bake 35 minutes. Remove from oven, drain off any fat, and evenly spread mashed potatoes over top.

Return casserole to oven and cook 25 to 30 more minutes, or until no pink remains in beef and potatoes are hot.

Amish Ham and Cheese Casserole

1 lb ham, cubed
1 med onion, chopped - optional
6 eggs
2 or 3 baked potatoes, diced into chunks*
2 cups shredded Cheddar and Colby Jack cheese
1 1/2 cups small curd cottage cheese

If you don't have baked potatoes, you can substitute 4
cups of frozen shredded hash browns, thawed.

Combine the ingredients in a large mixing bowl.
Transfer to a greased 13 in x 9 in baking dish.
Bake , uncovered , at 350 degrees F for 35- 40 min or
until set and bubbly.
 Let stand for 10 min. before cutting.

Amish Ham and Dumplings

Apples are the perfect go-along for almost any pork dinner, especially a smoked ham. And in this dish that originated with the Pennsylvania Dutch, we get an extra treat because the apples and pork are nestled in the same pot with puffy homemade dumplings.

What You'll Need:

    8 cups water
    1 (2 pounds) fully-cooked semi-boneless ham, cubed
    2 (6 ounce each) packages dried apples
    3 cups biscuit baking mix
    1 cup milk

What To Do:

In an 8-quart soup pot, combine the water, ham, and apples over medium-high heat and bring to a boil. Reduce the heat to low, cover, and simmer for 20 minutes.

In a medium-sized bowl, combine the baking mix and milk just until moistened.

Uncover the soup pot and carefully drop the batter by heaping tablespoonfuls into the soup pot, making 8 dumplings. Cook, uncovered, for 10 minutes. Cover and cook for 18 to 20 more minutes, or until the dumplings are fluffy and doubled in size.

Pennsylvania Dutch Chowchow

Chowchow is a Pennsylvania Dutch-style relish that you can easily make fresh to team with any of your main dish favorites. Our chopped, tangy Pennsylvania Dutch Chowchow is as down-home as can be.

What You'll Need:

    4 cups coarsely chopped celery
    1 cup coarsely chopped green bell pepper
    1 cup coarsely chopped red bell pepper
    1/2 cup coarsely chopped onion
    1/2 cup wine vinegar
    1 tablespoon mixed pickling spice
    1/3 cup sugar
    1 tablespoon salt
    1 teaspoon caraway seed

What To Do:

Place celery, green and red bell pepper, and onion in a large bowl; set aside.
In a saucepan, combine vinegar and pickling spice; bring mixture to a boil and boil 5 minutes.
 Strain mixture, then add sugar, salt, and caraway seed; pour over vegetables
Cover and refrigerate 24 hours before serving. Store in refrigerator up to one week.

Pennsylvania Dutch Green Beans

The garden fresh taste of our Amish-inspired Pennsylvania Dutch Green Beans that come with a hint of savory bacon, is sure to warrant second helpings at dinner

What You'll Need:

    6 bacon slices, chopped
    1 medium onion, chopped
    1 pound fresh green beans, cleaned, cut in half, and blanched
    2 large tomatoes, chopped
    1 teaspoon chopped fresh garlic
    1/2 teaspoon salt
    1/4 teaspoon black pepper

In a large skillet over medium-high heat, cook bacon and onion 6 to 8 minutes, or until bacon is crisp. Add the remaining ingredients and cook 8 to 10 minutes, or until beans are tender. Serve immediately.

Note: To blanch, cook the green beans in boiling water 3 to 5 minutes, drain, then plunge into cold water.

Amish Sausage Balls

Whether as a crowd-pleasing appetizer or as a robust main dish, the Amish country flavors come through as loud and clear as the sound of a horse and buggy coming down a country road.

What You'll Need:

1 pound Italian sausage, casing removed
1/2 cup plain bread crumbs
1/4 cup finely chopped onion
1 egg, beaten
2 teaspoons vegetable oil
1 1/2 cups ketchup
1/4 cup white vinegar
2 tablespoons soy sauce
1/2 cup light brown sugar

What To Do:
In a large bowl , combine sausage, bread crumbs, onion, and egg; mix well then form into 1/2-inch balls.
In a large skillet over medium-high heat, heat oil; brown sausage balls 5 minutes, stirring occasionally.
Meanwhile, in a medium bowl, combine remaining ingredients; mix well. Pour over sausage balls, cover, reduce heat to low, and simmer 20 to 25 minutes, or until no longer pink in center. Serve immediately.
Notes: These are traditionally served over rice or curly noodles. However, we also found these perfect as an appetizer served on toothpicks.
If you want to make these ahead of time, that's fine. Just reheat on a baking sheet in a 250 degree oven.

Dutch Noodles

Pennsylvania Dutch cooking has its roots in Germany, where many hearty recipes, like these comforting and flavorful buttery egg noodles, get their traditional taste from.

What You'll Need:

  1 (8-ounce) package medium egg noodles (see Note)
  1/4 cup (1/2 stick) butter
  2 teaspoons caraway seeds
  Juice of 1 lemon
  2 teaspoons chopped fresh parsley
  1 teaspoon salt
  1/4 teaspoon black pepper

What To Do:
Cook noodles according to package directions. Drain and place in a large serving bowl; keep warm.
 Meanwhile, in a medium saucepan, melt butter over medium heat. Add caraway seeds and saute 3 minutes. Stir in lemon juice, parsley, salt, and pepper.
Pour sauce over cooked noodles, and serve immediately.

Amish Dinner Rolls

2 cups milk
1 cup white sugar
1 cup butter
1½ tablespoons salt
2½ cups cold water
2 tablespoons yeast
4 eggs
12 cups bread flour

Heat milk to scalding. Add sugar, butter, and salt. Once butter is melted, add 1 cup of cold water and mix well. Add yeast and mix again. Add rest of water and eggs. Beat well, then add flour.

Let the dough rise to double in size. Knead it and let it rise again. Shape into small balls. Let them rise again. Bake at 325 degrees F for 20 minutes.

Makes about 4½ dozen rolls.

Amish-Style Mashed Potatoes

These potatoes are perfect for making ahead and using later, plus they've got more flavor than regular mashed potatoes.

    12 large potatoes
    1 package (8 ounce) cream cheese
    8 ounce sour scream
    1 teaspoon onion salt
    ¼ cup butter, browned
    paprika

Peel and cook potatoes in salt water until soft. Drain potatoes and add cream cheese, sour cream, and onion salt. Whip until fluffy. Spread in a 9×13 inch pan. Drizzle with butter and sprinkle with paprika. Bake at 350 degrees F for 1 hour. No gravy is needed. This can be frozen until ready to use.

Serves about 12 people.

HOT DUTCH POTATO SALAD

4 slices bacon
½ cup chopped onion
½ cup chopped green pepper
¼ cup vinegar
1 teaspoon salt
3 hard boiled eggs
2/8 teaspoon pepper
1 teaspoon sugar
1 egg
1 qt. hot, cubed, cooked potatoes
¼ cup grated raw carrot

Dice bacon and pan fry.
Add chopped onion and green pepper.
Cook 3 minutes.
Add vinegar, salt, pepper, sugar and beaten egg.
Cook slightly.
Add cubed potatoes, grated carrot and diced hard-cooked eggs.
Blend and serve hot.

AMISH BROCCOLI SALAD

1 large head broccoli, broken into small flowerettes
1/2 cups chopped onion
8 to 10 slices bacon
1 cup mayonnaise
1/4 to 1/2 cups sugar
2 to 3 tablespoons vinegar
1/2 cups raisins
1/2 cups nuts (optional)

Chop up bacon and fry until crisp.
Mix together mayonnaise, sugar, vinegar, bacon and raisins.
Pour over broccoli and onions. Mix well.
Let stand for an hour or more before serving.

SAUERBRATEN

2 inch thick piece of chuck, pot roast or tender boiling beef.

Place in dish or bowl and cover with solution of half vinegar and half water, put in two large onions sliced.

Do this two or three days before the meat is wanted.

On the day before it is to be cooked cut 3 or 4 slices of bacon into 1" pieces and chop fine 1 tablespoon of the onion which has been soaking in the vinegar.

Cut holes in the meat 1 or 2 inches apart and stuff bits of the bacon and chopped onion into the holes.

Put the meat back into the solution, add 1 tablespoon whole cloves and 1 teaspoon whole allspice.

Bake the meat as a pot roast in part of the solution, until tender. Use more of the solution, adding sugar to taste, in making the gravy which will be almost black.

AMISH HORSERADISH SAUCE RECIPE

* 2 tblsp. butter
* 2 tblsp. flour
* 1 cup milk
* ¼ cup grated horseradish
* ¼ tsp. dry mustard
* salt and pepper

Melt butter, remove from heat and stir in flour.
Add the milk gradually, stirring constantly, until mixture boils and thickens.
Add salt and pepper and cook for 3 minutes more.
Add the grated horseradish and dry mustard and blend well.
Keep hot in double boiler.
Serve on slices of roast beef, boiled beef or corned beef.

AMISH SCHNITZEL MEAT RECIPE

* 1½ lbs. veal steak cut in cubes
* 2 tblsp. shortening
* 2 tblsp. flour
* 1 cup tomato juice
* 2 carrots, diced
* 1 small onion, chopped fine
* Salt and pepper
* Flour

Dredge meat with flour and season.
Melt shortening (preferably bacon fat) and brown the meat in it.
Remove meat from the pan, stir in the flour and blend.
Add the tomato juice and stir well until mixture thickens.
Add meat, carrots and onion.
Cover closely and simmer for 45 minutes.

AMISH RECIPES FOR VEGETABLES

LANCASTER COUNTY BAKED CORN

To 1 cup of dried corn (ground in food chopper)
Pour on 2 cups of hot milk and let stand about an hour.
Add 2 eggs, 1 cup milk, 1 tablespoon butter, 2 table-
spoons sugar and salt to taste.
Bake ½ hour in oven of 350 to 360 degrees F.

AMISH SEVEN-MINUTE CABBAGE

2 cups milk
2 teaspoons flour
salt and pepper
1 tablespoon butter
2 cups chopped cabbage

Heat the milk to boiling. Add butter and the cabbage.
Cook seven minutes. Thicken with the flour, mixed with
a little cold water.

SCALLOPED SWEET POTATOES AND APPLES

6 medium-sized sweet potatoes
½ cup brown sugar
1½ cups sliced apples
4 tblsp. butter
½ tsp. salt
1 tsp. mace

Boil sweet potatoes until tender. Slice in ¼ inch pieces. Butter baking dish and put a layer of sweet potatoes in bottom, then a layer of apples. Sprinkle with sugar, salt and mace, and dot with butter. Repeat until dish is filled, having the top layer of apples. Bake in moderate oven (350 degrees F.) for 50 minutes.

AMISH SWEET POTATO CROQUETTES

1 pt. mashed sweet potatoes
1 tblsp. butter
1 tsp. salt
1 tblsp. sugar
1 egg white
bread crumbs

Mash sweet potatoes very fine and add salt, sugar and melted butter.

Shape into croquette rolls or patties and chill in the refrigerator for a half hour.

Roll in bread crumbs, dip in the egg white, slightly beaten, and in the crumbs again.

Bake in a shallow, greased baking dish for 20 minutes, in hot oven at 400 degrees F.

For a modern variation of this old recipe, place a marshmallow in the center of each with the potato mixture coating it completely.

AMISH SCHNITZEL BEANS

4 slices bacon
1 qt. string beans
3 medium onions, sliced
2 cups tomatoes, chopped
1 tsp. salt
¼ tsp. pepper
1 cup hot water

Dice the bacon and fry until crisp.
Slice the onions and fry until soft.
Cut the beans into small (1-inch) pieces and brown them
slightly with the bacon and onions.
Add the tomatoes, seasoning and boiling water.
Cover and cook very slowly until beans are tender.
Add water if necessary, so there will be a little sauce to
serve with the beans.

AMISH FRIED TOMATOES

4 tomatoes
3 tblsp. hot fat and butter
2 tblsp. brown sugar
flour
½ cup milk
salt and pepper

Cut large, solid, ripe tomatoes in ½ inch slices.
Dredge thickly with flour.
Fry quickly in 2 tablespoons of hot drippings or butter,
browning well on both sides.
Remove to serving platter, sprinkle with salt, pepper and
brown sugar. Keep warm.
Add 1 tablespoon of butter to the pan fryings and blend
in a tablespoon of flour.
Add the milk and cook, stirring constantly. It should be
about the consistency of thick cream.
Pour it over the tomatoes and serve.

AMISH PARSNIP PATTIES

6 or 7 parsnips
1 tablespoon butter or shortening
2 eggs
½ cup bread crumbs, dry
1 teaspoon sugar
½ teaspoon salt
little pepper
milk

Boil parsnips in salted water.
When soft, peel and remove the core then mash.
Add shortening, bread crumbs, salt, pepper, sugar and 1 egg and the white of the other, beaten.
Mix well and form into cakes.
Beat the remaining egg yolk with a little milk added.
Dip the cakes into the egg, roll in corn meal or bread crumbs and fry to a nice brown.

AMISH SCALLOPED POTATOES

6 potatoes, sliced
1 onion, chopped
2 tsp. salt
pepper
3 tblsp. butter
2 tblsp. flour
2 cups hot milk
¾ cup grated cheese

Melt butter in double boiler or sauce pan.
Add flour, seasoning and stir smooth.
Slowly add the hot milk stirring constantly.
When it thickens melt the grated cheese in the sauce. Into a buttered baking dish or casserole put layers of the sliced potatoes, onions and cheese sauce, repeating until all ingredients are used.

Bake in a moderate oven (350 degrees F.) for 1 hour.

MORAVIAN CHRISTMAS COOKIES

½ cup shortening
1 cup brown sugar
1 cup molasses
1 egg
4 cups flour
1 teaspoon cinnamon
1 teaspoon cloves
½ teaspoon nutmeg
1 teaspoon soda

Blend shortening, sugar and molasses.
Add beaten egg.
Sift dry ingredients and combine.
Mix well, roll out and cut in fancy shapes.
Bake at 350 degrees for 10 minutes.
When cool decorate with boiled icing.

OATMEAL COOKIES

3 c. Sugar
1 1/2 c. Lard
1 1/2 c. Raisins
2 1/2 c. Oatmeal
1/2 c. molasses (dark)
3 eggs, beaten
1 c. Peanuts
1 c. sour milk
2 tbsp. Soda
2 tbsp. baking powder
6 c. flour 1 tsp. each of nutmeg, cinnamon and salt

Grind raisins and peanuts.
Sift together flour, baking powder, nutmeg, cinnamon, salt.
Cut in lard, add sugar, oatmeal, raisins and peanuts and mix well again.
Dissolve soda in sour milk and add molasses and beaten eggs.
Chill one hour.
Using your hand, roll the dough into balls the size of a walnut and press slightly flat.
Beat two eggs and paint the top of the cookie with egg.
Bake at 375 degrees until golden brown.

DUTCH ALMOND COOKIES

1 cup shortening
½ cup white sugar
1 cup brown sugar
2 eggs
½ teaspoon vanilla
3 cups flour
¼ teaspoon cinnamon
¼ teaspoon nutmeg
¼ teaspoon soda
¼ teaspoon salt
½ cup ground blanched almonds

Cream shortening with white and brown sugar.
Add 2 eggs and work in the sifted dry ingredients.
Then add the chopped blanched almonds.
Shape dough into long rolls.
Roll in wax paper and store in cold place for 12 hours.
Slice thin and bake in hot oven.

CHOCOLATE CHIP CHRISTMAS COOKIES

1/2 c. shortening
1 c. sugar
2 large eggs
1/2 c. milk
2 1/2 c. flour
1 tsp. baking powder
3/4 tsp. baking soda (place in the milk)
12 oz chocolate chips
12 oz white baking chips
Sprinkles

Cream shortening and sugar.
Add eggs and milk with soda.
 Mix together and add baking powder. Gradually add flour and stir well.
Stir in chocolate chips or butterscotch chips.
Place on a greased cookie sheet about 1 teaspoon of dough.
Bake at 400 degrees until the edge is lightly brown.

To Decorate:
In small bowl, microwave 1/2 to 1 cup of the chips at a time (as needed), uncovered on Medium (50%) 2 to 3 minutes, stirring once, until chips can be stirred smooth.

Carefully dip each cookie halfway into melted chips; wipe off excess. Place on cooking parchment paper-lined tray; sprinkle with desired candies. Let stand until coating is firm, about 1 hour.

AMISH SAND TARTS

2 cups sugar
1 cup butter
4 eggs
flour

Work butter and part of the sugar together, then the remainder of the sugar and the eggs should be mixed in.
Use flour enough to make very stiff.
Roll thin, cut out in small squares, wet top with two eggs beaten, sprinkle with sugar, cinnamon and chopped almonds.
Bake in moderate oven, 10 minutes.

AMISH WALNUT KISSES

1 lb. sugar
6 egg whites
3 tablespoons flour
2 cups walnuts chopped

Beat egg whites until stiff and dry. Mix flour and sugar and fold in stiffly beaten egg whites. Add walnuts and bake in moderate oven, 375 degrees.

Sour Cream Cut-Out Christmas Cookies

Ingredients

1 cup (2 sticks) butter, softened
1½ cups sugar
3 large eggs, beaten
1 cup sour cream
2 tablespoons vanilla extract
3½ to 4 cups all-purpose flour
2 teaspoons baking powder
1 teaspoon baking soda

Instructions

Preheat the oven to 350°F. Lightly grease a baking sheet.
Cream the butter and sugar together in a large bowl.
Stir in the eggs, sour cream, and vanilla.
Combine the flour, baking powder, and baking soda in a medium bowl and stir with a whisk to blend.
Add the dry ingredients to the wet ingredients and stir until a soft, firm dough is formed.
Roll the dough out to a ½-inch thickness on a floured surface.
Use your favorite shaped cookie cutters to cut out the dough.
Place the shapes on the prepared pan.
Bake until golden brown around the edges, about 10 minutes.
Remove from the oven and let cool on the pan for 5 minutes, then transfer to wire racks to cool completely.

Frosting

¹/3 cup shortening
1 teaspoon vanilla
4 cups powdered sugar
½ cup milk
Food coloring (optional)

Colored sprinkles, for decorating (optional)
Chocolate chips, for decorating (optional)

Cream the shortening with the vanilla and 1 cup of the powdered sugar.
Gradually add the milk and the rest of the powdered sugar, beating constantly.
More powdered sugar can be added to give you your desired thickness.
Food coloring can also be added if you like.
Spread the frosting on the cookies and decorate with colored sprinkles or chocolate chips.
Let the frosting set before storing.

AMISH WALNUT ROCKS

1 cup butter
1½ cups brown sugar
3 eggs, beaten
1 tsp. soda
1½ tblsp. hot water
3 cups flour
½ tsp. salt
1 tsp. cinnamon
½ tsp. cloves
1½ cups chopped raisins
1 cup chopped walnuts

Cream butter and sugar and add the beaten eggs.
Dissolve soda in the hot water and add to the creamed mixture.
Sift flour, salt and spices twice and add half of it to mixture and mix thoroughly.
Combine chopped raisins and nuts with the other half and add to the dough.
Mix thoroughly and drop by teaspoonfuls onto greased baking sheets spaced a couple of inches apart.
Bake in moderate oven (350-f) for 12 to 15 minutes.

LEBKUCHEN

This is an old recipe for an old time Christmas favorite.

1½ cups flour
1 tblsp. cinnamon
½ tsp. nutmeg
½ tsp. cloves, ground
½ tsp. cream of tartar
2 eggs, beaten
1 cup dark brown sugar
1/8 lb. citron, chopped fine
1/8 lb. almonds, chopped

Sift the flour, cinnamon, nutmeg, cloves and cream of tartar.
Mix the sugar and beaten eggs thoroughly.
Combine with the flour mixture, add citron and the almonds.
Roll out on floured board, ¼ inch thick.
Place on a greased cookie sheet and bake in moderate oven (350-f) for 15 minutes.
Cut into squares or diamonds while still warm. Ice thinly with plain white or lemon frosting.

JOIN THE AMISH ON FACEBOOK:
https://www.facebook.com/groups/visittheamish

Amish stories, pictures, news, recipes and more.
Talk a walk in Amish Country on the internet.
http://www.visittheamish.com/

www.ingramcontent.com/pod-product-compliance
Lightning Source LLC
Chambersburg PA
CBHW030532290526
45786CB00004B/1698